I0759145

I'm very grateful to you, my dear Colorist, for choosing this coloring book and I hope you will enjoy every page of it as much as I did while creating it. Every single page was created with love and positive vibes of classic music.

I'm sure that you will get excellent coloring masterpieces. Would you like to share them with me? If you share your art-work on social networks, add a hash tag **#floralmandalasbook** so I could see them and proudly give you a huge LIKE and a couple of smiley faces :)

Thank you for supporting my art-work. I would really appreciate if you could leave a **little feedback (review)** to encourage me to keep up a good work and to grow further as an artist.

FULL DIGITAL COPY OF THE INTERIOR :)

Input this link **https://goo.gl/m9xjR4** into your web browser (pay an attention to upper case letters). It will lead you to the Dropbox-cloud-platform to get a Digital copy of all 50-Floral-Mandalas in PDF format file. Just tap "Download" button and you'll have it on your PC. All Mandalas are on a regular white background and can be printed as a one file, in small groups or just one by one.

In case you'll have a problem with this file or the will to contact me directly, please write me an email to: **dv.design15@gmail.com**

I wish you to have a great time with this book :)

Sincerely yours, Elinorka.